Dear Parents and Educators,

Welcome to Penguin Young Readers! As parents and educators, you know that each child develops at his or her own pace—in terms of speech, critical thinking, and, of course, reading. Penguin Young Readers recognizes this fact. As a result, each Penguin Young Readers book is assigned a traditional easy-to-read level (1–4) as well as a Guided Reading Level (A–P). Both of these systems will help you choose the right book for your child. Please refer to the back of each book for specific leveling information. Penguin Young Readers features esteemed authors and illustrators, stories about favorite characters, fascinating nonfiction, and more!

Home Address: ISS
International Space Station

LEVEL **4**

GUIDED READING LEVEL **O**

This book is perfect for a **Fluent Reader** who:
- can read the text quickly with minimal effort;
- has good comprehension skills;
- can self-correct (can recognize when something doesn't sound right); and
- can read aloud smoothly and with expression.

Here are some **activities** you can do during and after reading this book:
- Using a Glossary: A glossary, like a dictionary, tells you what words mean. Look at the words and their definitions in the glossary at the back of this book. Then write an original sentence for each word.
- Captions: Some of the photos in this book have captions. A caption is a little explanation of the photograph. Find the photos that do not have captions. Using the facts in the book, write captions on sticky paper, and stick them on the appropriate photos.

Remember, sharing the love of reading with a child is the best gift you can give!

—Bonnie Bader, EdM
  Penguin Young Readers program

*Penguin Young Readers are leveled by independent reviewers applying the standards developed by Irene Fountas and Gay Su Pinnell in *Matching Books to Readers: Using Leveled Books in Guided Reading,* Heinemann, 1999.

Dedicated to the students at McKinley School in Santa Barbara, California. May all your dreams come true!—JB

PENGUIN YOUNG READERS
An Imprint of Penguin Random House LLC

Smithsonian

This trademark is owned by the Smithsonian Institution and is registered in the U.S. Patent and Trademark Office.

Smithsonian Enterprises:
Christopher Liedel, President
Carol LeBlanc, Senior Vice President, Education and Consumer Products
Brigid Ferraro, Vice President, Education and Consumer Products
Ellen Nanney, Licensing Manager
Kealy Gordon, Product Development Manager

Andrew K. Johnston, Geographer, Center for Earth and Planetary Studies, National Air and Space Museum, Smithsonian

Photo credits: page 48 © shirophoto/Thinkstock; All other photos courtesy of NASA.

Library of Congress Cataloging-in-Publication Data is available.

ISBN 978-0-448-48709-0 (pbk)
ISBN 978-0-448-48769-4 (hc)

10 9 8 7 6 5 4 3 2 1
10 9 8 7 6 5 4 3 2 1

Smithsonian

Home Address: ISS
International Space Station

by James Buckley Jr.

Penguin Young Readers
An Imprint of Penguin Random House

Welcome Home

Good-bye, Earth! Hello, space! This huge machine will be your home for the next three months. The International Space Station, or ISS, flies 205 miles (330 km) above the Earth. It travels more than five miles (eight km) per second. That's one spin around our planet every 90 minutes!

Fifteen nations worked together to build the ISS. It took more than 10 years to finish. The ISS is bigger than a football field. It's the world's largest high-flying, fast-moving house!

First step on your mission: reaching the ISS! After about six hours, your rocket ship from Earth has nearly arrived at the space station. While you're on the rocket, you can take off your helmet. But when it's time to dock, helmets are on!

A smaller rocket connects with the ISS. When you glide onto the space station, you're greeted by an astronaut. There is always someone home at the ISS!

On the way to the launchpad

Good Space Morning!

After the flight from Earth, your first day on the ISS begins. Check it out— wake-up music! The **controllers** on Earth send up your favorite tunes. Some astronauts make requests. Others get a surprise, like a rock tune with their name in it!

In space, the sun comes "out" about every 90 minutes, so when does the day begin? You'll live on the same schedule as the controllers on Earth.

Time to brush your teeth. On the ISS, people live and work close together. Good breath is a big plus! After you brush, just swish and swallow. There's no spitting in space. You can even use your favorite brand of toothpaste. (Don't let the cap float away!)

Need to wash up? There are no showers here, only sponge baths. To wash your hair, you use a special shampoo. You don't need water—just squirt, scrub, and wipe!

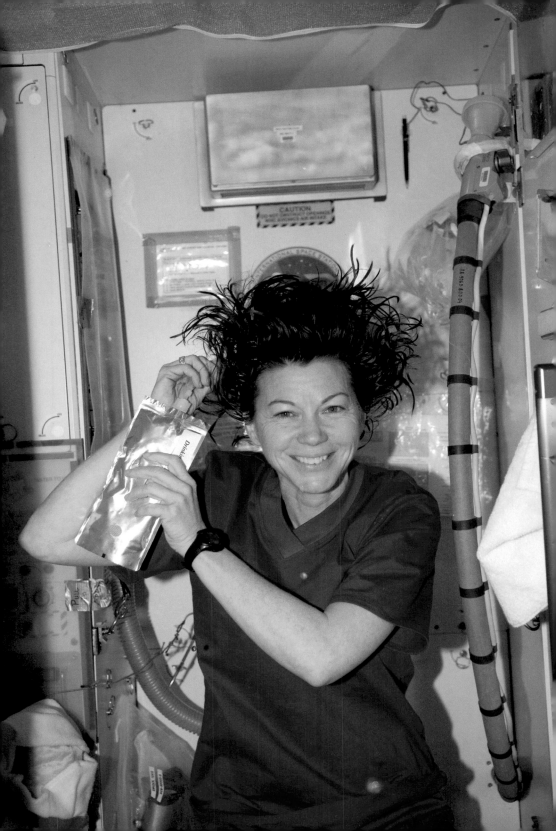

Everybody has to "go" . . . even in space. Using the toilet in the ISS is a bit tricky. The space toilet is designed to keep liquids and solids from floating away. Liquid waste goes down a tube designed for men or women. For solid waste, you sit on a small seat in a compartment. A vacuum below sucks in while you let everything out.

Afterward, wash your hands with **disposable** cloths like the hand wipes you use on Earth.

Like everything else on the ISS, eating takes a bit more work than it does on Earth. Here, most of your food is **dehydrated**. That means all the water has been taken out. So you add a bit of water, stir, and eat.

This is an international space station, so you might have food from different countries. Russian **cosmonauts** bring great spicy lamb soup. The Japanese crew has left behind fish soup for you. And there are always plenty of tortillas— some astronauts fill them with peanut butter and jelly!

Liquids can only be taken in with straws. An escaping blob of floating orange juice could damage ISS gear. And no crumbs, please!

Adding water to a dehydrated lunch

After breakfast, you can put on your clothes for the day. You can't waste water washing clothes on the space station. Instead, you'll put on new clothes every two or three days. The tricky part is dressing while floating in zero gravity!

You won't wear shoes, either. Since you'll be floating around, your feet might touch pieces of gear. So soft slippers make your feet comfy and safe!

After everyone is ready, it's time for work. Each morning, the ISS crew gathers to plan the day. Part of the fun of living on the space station is working with people from other countries. You have to study languages to live in space. People could be speaking English, Russian, Japanese, or French!

The station commander makes sure the crew knows their jobs for the day. Up to six full-time crew members can be on board. When a spaceship is docked, that can add three more people!

After the morning meeting, the workday begins.

Astronauts at Work

It's very important that the ISS works properly. The crew checks all the space station's gear and machines every day. You might have to change an air filter. Even the toilet might need some attention to work perfectly. Just like in a home on Earth, there is always something that needs fixing!

If you use tools, you have to make sure they don't float too far away. You can hook your feet in straps if you need to stay in one place while you work.

Like most of the ISS crew, you are also a scientist. Living in space gives you a chance to do important experiments. Your tests can help people on Earth!

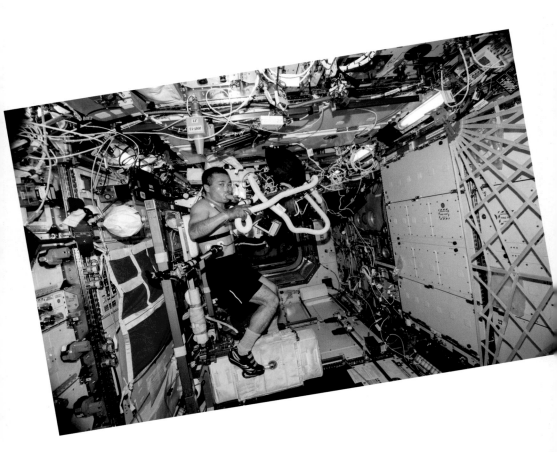

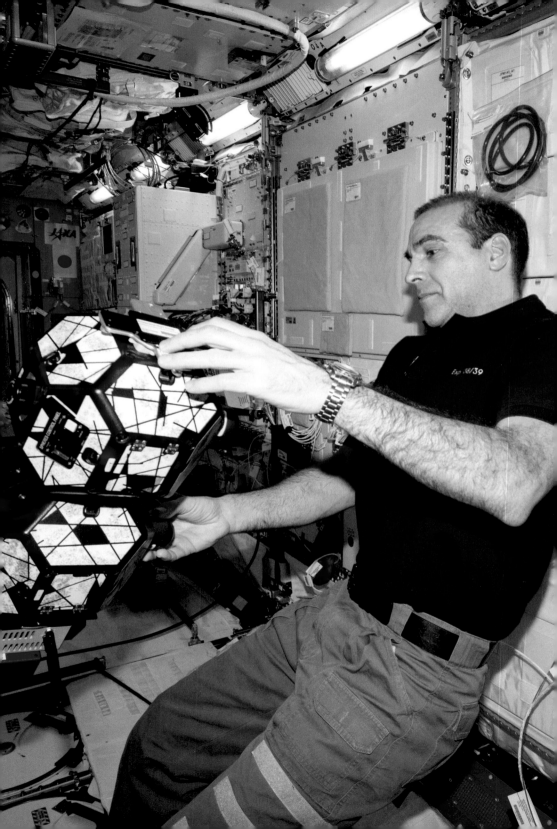

ISS studies have led to the invention of new medicines. Crews have learned how human bodies live in space. They have observed more about our **galaxy**. They have even grown plants and watched animals adapt to space.

It takes dozens of computers to run the International Space Station. They help you perform and record experiments, communicate with Earth, or operate the ISS. Making sure the computers are all working is a big part of your day.

You might even be the ISS computer expert. One of the crew is in charge of installing and repairing computer parts and **programming**. He or she works with a team on Earth to keep things humming along.

Nearly all your time is spent inside the ISS. But sometimes, you get to step outside . . . into space! You put on a huge space suit. This provides air and protects you from the cold of space. You connect yourself to the ISS with strong cords. Then you float!

A space walk is not playtime. Each space walk is like a mini mission. You need to have the right tools and training, and then get the job done. That might mean replacing a part, fixing a **solar panel**, or changing a **window shield**. It also means using tools while wearing huge, bulky gloves!

The best part about a space walk is the view! As you float hundreds of miles above the Earth, the giant globe floats below you. You can see clouds and continents, rivers and rain forests. Can you find your home country?

The ISS crew often sits in a place called the **cupola**. It's like an observation post inside the space station. The pictures they take from there let us all share in the wonder.

Chores? In Space?

You have chores at home, you have chores in space! The whole crew works together to keep their space home tidy. No mops, though. Use hand wipes to clean surfaces. Vacuuming removes floating dust or crumbs from the air.

In a crowded space like the ISS, everything has a place. You have to make sure that all the gear is **stowed** properly and tied down. You never know when you might need it! Velcro is your best friend.

Teamwork is important on the space station. Everyone has to work together and get along. You can't go out somewhere to get away from one another.

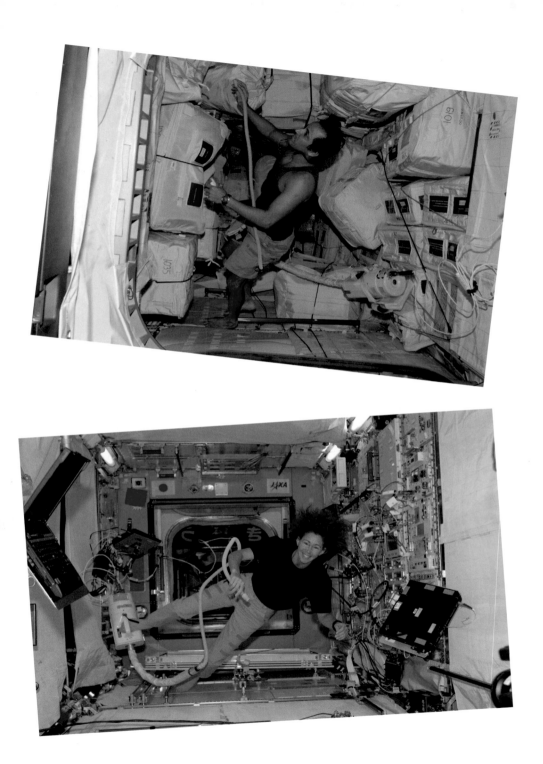

The ISS is usually on **autopilot**. But it still needs a driver. You have to practice steering, just in case. In an area called the central post, you look at a computer screen. It shows all the controls. You can make the space station rotate slowly or change direction. It's important for the ISS to keep the right **orientation** with the Earth and the sun. Why do you think that is? Here's a hint: The space station runs on solar energy.

You can also practice using one of the station's robot arms. They can work in space while you sit safely inside!

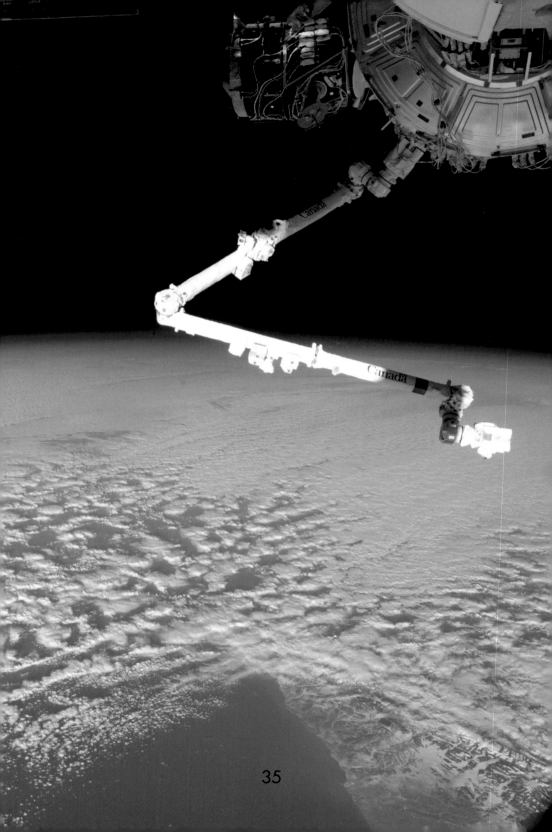

Your muscles won't work as hard in space. After all, you're just floating! To make sure your muscles stay strong during your long stay, you exercise every day. You can pedal on a machine that is like a bicycle without wheels. You can strap yourself in to a treadmill. The straps will keep you from floating away!

A special machine called the A-RED helps you "lift weights." Since everything is weightless in space, you're really pushing against a machine, not raising heavy things.

Today, you've got some special work to do. You float in front of a camera and do a video chat with students on Earth. They ask questions, and you use a microphone to answer them . . . live from space!

One student wants to know if you ever need a haircut in space. After all, you'll be up there for months! "Yes," you answer. "We have clippers on board. We attach a vacuum hose to them so the cut hair doesn't float around!"

Good Night, Float Tight!

After a hard day's work, it's time for dinner. First, pick your packaged dinner. How about turkey tonight? If you want potatoes, too, you have to add water (carefully!) and then heat. Many ISS crew members like to add hot sauce. In space, food seems not to taste as good, and the spiciness helps. Since you have just arrived with fresh supplies, there are some apples and oranges to eat. Enjoy them now. With only a small fridge, you won't have fresh fruit for long.

When the work on the station is all finished, it's time to relax. You might float around and read a book. You can listen to music on your headphones. Some crew members read and send e-mail. It's a great way to keep up with faraway family and friends.

You might take a break for a concert. Some astronauts have brought musical instruments. They had to learn how to move their hands in zero gravity to make music!

Sewing in space

Finally, it's time for bed. Well, time for sleep, anyway. You can spend the night in a sleeping bag stuck to a wall. Or you can slip into one of the space station sleeping pods. A fan will blow near your head. That pushes fresh air over your face. Otherwise, the air you breathe out would cover your face like a bubble. Some crew members wear earplugs, too. The ISS machines never sleep, so there is always humming, buzzing, and whirring going on around you.

When you fall asleep, you might just dream that you're floating in space.

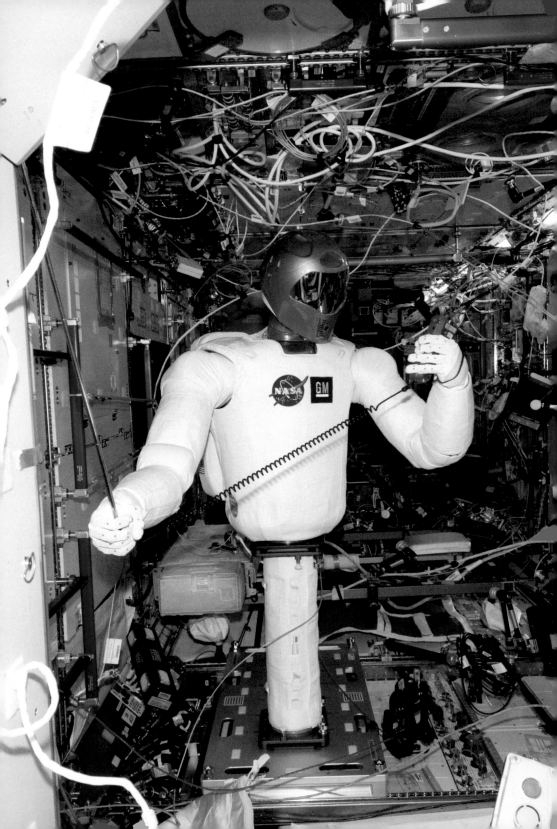

Now it is "night" on the ISS. You have been around the world more than seven times since you woke up!

While you sleep, one crew member is hard at work. He's called Robonaut. He's a robot astronaut! Robonaut helps keep ISS systems working while the human crew rests.

Good night, Robonaut.

Good night, ISS.

autopilot: a computer system that controls movement

controllers: people who work on the ground to help the ISS with its mission

cosmonaut: name for space travelers from Russia

cupola: a small, round part of a building that sticks up or out

dehydrate: to remove water from a solid

disposable: can be thrown away

galaxy: a system of planets, stars, and other space bodies

orientation: the position of something in relation to something else

programming: instructions that make a computer do its job

solar panel: a device that takes in solar energy to be converted into electricity

stowed: put away in the right place

window shield: a panel on the ISS that covers a window to keep out the sun's heat and light